AF654691

US &I

AISHWARYA BORA

US & I

AISHWARYA BORA

PAPER TOWNS
PUBLISHERS

First published by
Papertowns Publishers 72,
Vishwanath Dham Colony,
Niwaru Road, Jhotwara,
Jaipur, 302012

US & I
Copyright © Aishwarya Bora, 2021

ISBN Print Book - 978-81-947125-8-9

All rights reserved. No part of this book may be reproduced or transmitted in any form or by any means, electronic or mechanical, including photocopying, recording, or by an information storage and retrieval system—except by a reviewer who may quote brief passages in a review to be printed in a magazine, newspaper, or on the Web—without permission in writing from the copyright owner.

Although the author and publisher have made every effort to ensure the accuracy and completeness of information contained in this book, we assume no responsibility for errors, inaccuracies, omissions, or any inconsistencies herein. Any slights on people, places, or organizations are unintentional.

Cover Design by Amit Ramchandani
Email: amitr18x@gmail.com

ACKNOWLEDGMENT

2020 seemed as a bad year, but it wasn't that bad. To pass time in the lockdown, I started writing poems and short stories. I had no idea I would ever combine my poems into a book. 2020 gave me the idea to do so. When the script of my book was ready, I was really surprised that I wrote a poetry book. One of the best moments of 2020 for me, my liking towards writing increased immensely in 2020. I'm grateful to my family and friends for pushing me to follow my passion. Indirectly all of them helped me discover my passion for writing. I would really like to thank Papertowns India for giving me such an opportunity.

SYNOPSIS

'Us & I' is about love, pain and self-love. When love breaks us, it's the love within us that helps us grow. It's about feeling all the emotions and letting go of the darkness within us. To heal yourself, you need to give time to yourself. Love yourself each and every day, so that it's easy to love someone else. The feeling of love will give all the happiness to you. Will make you stronger and will give you peace too.

I want you to,
walk with me in the dark,
to hold on my tears,
to push me to fight,
but not fight for me,
and to love my emptiness,
I'm waiting for you,
where are you?
To create the space for you.

The forest within me,
blazing with fire,
you poured water drop by drop,
calmed me down,
you filled me with hope,
a rebirth to my soul,
to be little purer,
to love an angel like you.

I want us to be ‘we’,
let’s leave the ‘I’ behind,
walking together in our new phase,
drilling a way in the chaos,
to stand and fight as one,
to the world out there,
I loudly say,
“We love us.”

I knew you were waiting,
for my yes,
but fear had gulped me up,
it felt like my past was running behind me,
I don't have the strength to heal again,
I have tested you enough,
my heart says yes,
but my mind is still a mess.

It had become dusty,
you wiped the dust on my heart,
slowly and steadily.
I could see you,
your reflection could be seen in my
heart,
now my heart beats twice,
one for you and one for me,
filling it with your magical love,
you conquered me.

Our eyes talked,
but our mouths were shut,
each day the same story,
I couldn't resist,
words didn't come out,
but this time, when I saw you,
I gathered all the energy,
to say, "My eyes loved yours and now I
love you"

I was just running,
running behind you,
trying to catch hold of you,
in my blindness of love,
I couldn't see,
your toxic heart,
which just wanted fun,
but I opened the blindfold,
saw you clearer,
and ran,
this time to save myself,
to save my purity.

Wind is sweeping me off,
left a hurricane in me,
storm of pain hit me hard,
I craved for you,
but you broke me up,
I lost me,
needed to stand to love,
to love myself this time,
just to be mine.

In the world of false,
I found a truth, beautifully dark,
your heart gleamed through your words,
brown eyes looked at me with grace,
I wanted to go deeper,
to reflect you in me,
you being with me is bliss.

You upraised me in your love,
my body trusted your touch,
you created comfort within me,
your light bloomed me like a flower,
you filled my flaws with love,
made my eyes to see you everywhere,
you gave me warmth,
blessed to be in your life.

Coffee in bed is the way,
of my morning love,
caring for you,
the whole day,
helping you clean,
is my evening love,
putting you in bed,
with hugs and kisses,
is my night love,
to take away all your tiredness,
and let you in peaceful sleep,
with the dreams of us,
is the way I spell love.

To the rain of pureness,
growing the heart strong,
mind twirling in your thoughts,
your presence absorbed in me,
gliding in your love,
embracing your flaws,
you completely stole me,
with all my heart.

I wanted more,
larger place in your life,
most of your attention,
I was tired,
just being your friend,
I loved you more,
as the time passes,
still the ray of hope,
being loved by you,
tinkles in my heart.

You make me feel safe,
you look deep in me,
my body loves your touch,
but I'm scared,
What if our secret is out?
I can't lose my heart,
my tears won't be enough to get you
back,
if you aren't mine,
I'm not fine.

The awakening of my dream,
your curls brushing your face,
your face glowing up like a sun,
fair skin shined your heart,
your beauty captured my eyes,
it was like an ocean,
just endless,
looking at each other's eyes,
we ran,
leaving our footprints on the sand.

Sometimes
love is salty
to taste but
sweet to feel
just like a meal
made with love.

You stitched my broken pieces,
embraced all the stitches,
replaced pain with love,
effortlessly healed me up,
brought back my shine,
made me look pretty,
and made me love me more than
enough.

Your scent is my fragrance,
you are my power,
holding you in my arms gives me
strength,
a little closer each time,
my heart starts to sing, "You're the one,
You're the one, Let's hold hands and
have fun."

You gave me wounds,
you gave me scars,
I found your love in all,
ached each second,
but when I saw in your eyes,
all my sufferings drained out,
I just wanted you near me,
but you pushed me away always,
I sank in your love,
my love for you was a pain for me.

I build myself on your desires,
ran to complete your expectations,
took efforts for your happiness,
I uplifted my bar in the wrong direction,
only for your love,
your love becomes poison,
but I still drank it in hope,
hope of being loved back,
I cursed myself with your love,
which drowned me in the dark.

As I dwell into the clutches of the world,
my head is hanging with problems,
taste of misery on my tongue,
my body is losing the power of
resilience,
my footprints leave the pain,
want to bury myself,
to be reborn with strength,
to live life with a new length,
to discover the love,
within me for me.

White and black
were the only colours.
Now I have red added to it.

I love to tease you,
listening to my words,
your expressions rapidly change,
your face turning red,
shit man, you look so cute!
Firing back on me,
we both end my laughing,
this is the way we live,
growing old with more laughter.

From our first teeth,
our journey picked up,
from fighting all day long,
we didn't realise we fell in love.
Today we are taking our vows,
a promise of lifetime,
to grow together,
to hold you till my last breath,
and to love you and me.

Your voice is roaming in my mind,
it feels like the best music,
I can hear it all day long,
it is the only thing that keeps me going,
I lost you to the problems of my life,
I gained success,
but the failure of losing you,
I still wish you being with me,
waiting till the moment I die.

Your world was illusionary,
everything happened at your desire,
you curved me as you want,
So that in the real world you can flaunt
me,
but the light of the real world,
pulled me back from you,
your love was just an illusion,
just a fake fusion.

I hate you,
we started by this,
time changed its game,
I started liking you,
I loved when you annoyed me,
I didn't want to fight anymore,
I just wanted you to be mine,
I dreamed about it every night,
but I want,
to turn my dreams into reality.
So, I ask you,
Will you be mine?

You surprised me,
by changing you for me,
just for me to be fond of you,
to give you a place,
where my love is filled,
you cared each moment,
even when you changed,
today I know I deserve you,
the whole you.

I was running away,
I knew what you meant to me,
tears shed every night,
in accepting the fact,
that you were no more mine,
I know we loved each other,
with all our passion,
but we were not meant to be together,
maybe in some other life.

Unloving you,
felt impossible,
until and unless,
I soaked our memories,
with no regrets,
made a new place,
to welcome,
new adventures of life.

The bad in you attracted my eyes,
to see the good in you,
to nurture it,
to keep it growing,
till the end.

Second, minutes, hours, days, months,
all passed by,
your love made me learn, value of me,
value of you, value of us,
how to keep it safe,
in this growing world.

Let us both sail,
up and down along the waves,
direction
given by the wind,
how hard the water hits us,
we both will standstill.

You are my moon,
in the dark sky,
I'm your star,
always beside you.

Being with you,
for years,
I experienced,
all the different emotions,
their shades,
went in deep,
and discovered,
many more colours,
you possess.

The night is young,
our love is shining,
hand in hand we are walking,
moonlight giving us a way,
our darkness fading with the moon,
we bloomed in the sunlight,
together and strong,
for the love of us and just us.

How far I can see,
I can just see you,
you marked your place in my life,
your thought makes me smile,
come on baby,
please come back to me,
I miss you more,
the water of the ocean will be less to
describe.

My heart rained with your love,
air around just smelled like you,
water tasted sweet as you,
every minute passed thinking about
you, memories together were the best,
separation from you is dragging me
down, please come back and hold my
hand,
I promise no drop of tear to your eyes,
just a smile always,
I wanted to walk miles with you,
please come back and look in my eyes,
I regret my words,
which broke your heart,
my love please come back.

I envy death,
hundred candles are melted,
2400 hours are passed out,
but still your presence is felt,
I want to forget you,
But you just come back as always,
I envy death for taking you,
I miss you in my every thought,
you're the one who heals my heart.

Hair wanted to be set free,
eyes wanted to watch the blue sky,
backbone needed to lie down,
my skin needed the touch of the wind,
no pain, no gain,
just a pause from noise and thoughts,
a shot of calmness by the gun,
I just needed this one,
to regain myself.

You put your hand in my body,
snatched my heart out,
healed all my cracks,
your undefined love,
soaked you in me,
my heart pumps blood for you,
as a symbol of love from me to you.

Your hand entangled in my hair,
my lips touched yours,
a deep breath of love,
my skin feeling you,
mind soaking you in my heart,
each droplet filling me with you,
it's just you and only you,
a bubble of us surrounding us.

I know your heart is chaos,
but just trying to balance each thread,
for you to walk free,
shedding all my love for her,
to make you pure again,
to bring the light back,
So, you smile and spread it all around.

You are in my every thought,
every emotion,
everywhere around me,
I can't let myself out of you,
I fear you will come back,
to break me into parts again,
I can't handle your love any more,
just leave me alone,
to my path.

Come and take me,
to the highest point,
as high as our love,
from there,
we will show the world,
how beautiful love is,
how it shaped us,
and how we smile together,
every second of our life.

I don't want
an expensive ring
I want you to
promise me
not to break my heart
till we last.

I don’t want me,
to be your distraction,
in your growth,
that will make me,
guilty of my love,
I want to be a help,
where my love and me,
are part of it.

Let's paint the sky,
in our colours,
our memories,
of loving each other.
So, when we look up,
we see us.

You're walking away,
can't even catch your hand,
you left me with a gift,
memories and love,
falling apart in the distance,
coming closer in the heart,
closing my eyes and remembering you,
tears in my eyes,
smile on my face,
gazing at the dark sky to find my star,
but you're so far.

I want to feel the sunlight, touch and play
with it,
want to hug the wind and fly with its
direction wherever it goes,
want the moon to tell me, “Hey!! Kiddo,
don’t worry, everything will be fine.
Come here and spent the night with me and
my
shining stars”.
To skate through all the planets like never
before, to talk with the different masses in
the space,
to live as it is my last day in the universe,
feeling all the energies and busting out like
shining stars in the dark sky,
to feel myself like never before.

About the Author

Ups and down in my career made me discover myself. It took time for me to discover me,but it was worth the time. I fought battles with myself to bring out the real me. I found my passion. Slowly and gradually,

I start moving towards it. 'Us & I' is a symbol of my passion and a small step towards it. There's more to learn.

To stay in touch with me; here is my Instagram Id and my Email Id.

Instagram Id: _aishwarya31
Email id: bora.aishwarya502@gmail.com